LOVE AND THE SOUL

Phoenix Poets

A SERIES EDITED BY ALAN SHAPIRO

Love and the Soul

Alan Williamson

THE UNIVERSITY OF CHICAGO PRESS *Chicago and London*

Alan Williamson is professor of English at the University of California, Davis. He is the author of two previous books of poetry, *Presence* (1983) and *The Muse of Distance* (1988); and three critical works, *Pity the Monsters* (1974), *Introspection and Contemporary Poetry* (1984), and *Eloquence and Mere Life* (1994).

The University of Chicago Press, Chicago 60637
The University of Chicago Press, Ltd., London
© 1995 by The University of Chicago
All rights reserved. Published 1995
Printed in the United States of America
04 03 02 01 00 99 98 97 96 95 1 2 3 4 5

ISBN: 0–226–89932–2 (cloth)
0–226–89933–0 (paper)

Library of Congress Cataloging-in-Publication Data

Williamson, Alan (Alan Bacher), 1944–
     Love and the soul / Alan Williamson.
          p.   cm.—(Phoenix poets)
     I. Title.   II. Series.
     PS3573.I45623L68   1995
     811'.54—dc20   95-8679
                                      CIP

♾ The paper used in this publication meets the minimum requirements of the American National Standard for Information Sciences—Permanence of Paper for Printed Library Materials, ANSI Z39.48-1984.

Contents

Acknowledgments

I would like to thank the editors of the following publications, in which the poems listed first appeared:

AGNI: "November and December," "The Minoan Distance"

American Poetry Review: "Deb's Dream about Pavese," "Highway Restaurant," "Toward the New Year"

Antioch Review: "Two People in Two Houses on a Hill," "Wires at Inspiration Point"

Blind Donkey: "Tidepools" (vol. 15, no. 1)

Boston Phoenix Literary Section: "The Author Reconsiders"

Boston Review: "Rilke's Argument with Don Giovanni"

California Quarterly: "Forest Street"

Jacaranda Review: "The Etruscan Couple in the Villa Giulia"

Northeast Corridor: "The Moments," "Your Forest-Moonlight Picture" (vol. 2, no. 1)

Paris Review: "Love and the Soul"

Ploughshares: "Unanticipated Mirrors"

Southwest Review: "Fire and Flood"

Virginia Quarterly Review: "Domestic Architecture," "Enthusiasm," "Letter to Santa Fe," "Wide-Angle Shot: *Return to Snowy River*"

ZYZZYVA: "For My Daughter, Leaving"

I am grateful to the John Simon Guggenheim Memorial Foundation, the MacDowell Colony, and the University of California at Davis, which sweetened my sabbatical in 1992–93, for indispensable time. And to my friends, too many to name, who have affected here a line, there an order of stanzas, there the order of the entire book.

LOVE AND THE SOUL

I

The Author Reconsiders

Of course I look back on the first parts with amazement.
Adultery is a coffee-table book. As for being *angry*
that your first, dream-darkened choice
didn't mesh just right; and found someone else who did . . .
Then that other stuff: *A Sad Heart at the Singles Bar?*
But perhaps a feeling is measured by the newness
brought to it: the walk past the crest, by the freeways—
that hunger of bare hills
eating the world to origin and finality—
were what they seemed, if only because I had never
lived so purely, outside the rules. But the old life stayed—
it too possibility, it too unlived.
If one friend speaks of "certain old arrangements
that don't hold good any more,"
another friend says, "They say you did the worst thing,
you, the 'innocent' one, bringing her there
in the house with your wife, pretending to talk about poetry . . ."
What I mind most, in these pages,
is having said so little to explain
why things darken so quickly, between men and women,
and not just in marriage; how soon,
after the sheer balloon-like luck of the party,
they're so huge to each other, niggled-at, unappeasable . . .
The man, we're told, all fist, drawn in from the sensed cold
until every thought is counterargument;
the woman hammering and hammering, so unshakeable

her sense of powerlessness, at his ear, like a locked door in a dream;
her dread of being overshadowed; his conviction
that, whatever outsiders may think, the dark strike-back
she's drawn from him at last is, as she'll say, his true
nature unveiled, distilled; all that leads back to
nolo contendere, that odd plea in law courts
that gives up the chance to look innocent, pays the penalty
whatever it is, sure it's the smaller cost . . .

Epilogue

We will not see the gardens
of old age.
They were made for us,

but we got there too soon,
carrying our coffee cups into them
after breakfast, or at rest amid the daylong books,

with the fixed smiles
of those
who have outworn love's aggressions,

to see the other gardens
where love
is beyond aggression.

We were so strangely
afraid to enter them together,
as if, for all our tenderness,

we had married each other
in revenge, to destroy some hope in each other,
as only siblings

or parents should know enough to destroy.
Was that what we hid from, under
small names—

sharp, biting, moping but
consolable creatures? (Though yours
were always smaller, always slipping away . . .)

Lately I dreamed
we were lying, very ill, on our backs in an old house,
both of us

trying to die at the same moment.
There was no
terror, only an enormous exulting

sadness; then the instants, the itching
uncertainty, how one managed that, *to die* . . .
I thought of the other

dream, after the ultrasound, when our daughter
became real to us
(for weeks she bore her report name, "Normal Female"),

how we had bought a huge house
on the island
we walked parallel to for a mile, along the bayside

beach, picking up husks of horseshoe crabs,
that one happy weekend, shadowed
by your bleeding, the fear of miscarriage

(the happiness realized most under the shadow).
And in the house, a young man,
his arms raised and bunched, seemed to strive with the air

on the upper floor; while on the lower
old people, in a whiteness
of photos or cataracts, rocked and looked out to sea.

Would the dead
have been in it so much, if we
had known better how to fan the life in each other?

We had always defined ourselves
as the only people
capable of understanding each other's near-incapacity

for life, so well it alchemized
into that warmed, awkwardly brisk capacity
we displayed to the world.

That I—that we—had produced life
was like
the white unbreathable air of the upper ridges;

I quivered, the whole lung burned with it, I fell . . .
Not sayable. Underground
blankness. When I emerged from it

you had discovered, you
thought, that you no longer loved me.
I climbed out of it

daily facing your vision of the worst in me
as Dante pulls himself
out of Hell by the matted tufts on Satan's thighs,

only thinking he's descending
further, until at
last he stands free beneath the sky.

We seemed to have some agreement
that I would eventually
do the worst possible thing to you—

your dream-future
aloneness, flung in my face
yet yearned for . . .

For me, your anger,
read back, proffered a reason
why I could not—or would not—feel wholly released with you.

So in all things that descend
there is an in-
extricability, a pair of toothed gears, surface

causing surface causing . . .
—That New Year's, when the woman I left you for
dismissed me by letter,

Joanne said in the bar, "I don't think men and women
are meant to have relationships any more."
I thought of the computers

I was told about in Chicago,
that can be used but not explained, because their inner connections
will soon go faster than the speed of light.

—So the reactions fall from us,
understood, often, before we can even perceive them,
let alone call them back;

yet seeming so willful, sometimes, it takes years
to see they may have been
the only ones we could possibly have had . . .

There was so much that was ordinary and good between us.
I found that out the summer
I wanted to extirpate it, make it nothing,

and then looked up and
saw you: how your smile altered your face; your dogged
little-girl application, over the hooks and barbs

of Hebrew—a new language every summer . . .
And over you the books
you'd left for me to range, in so many houses . . .

That same August, my not-quite-lover
wrote me, "Thinking of leaving him, I still
ask his permission to go to bed at ten . . ."

—Like trying to chop a tree down, root by root,
that hopeless, until the last
frighteningly, emptily easy pull . . .

Even our first talk of this parting wandered
into memories of Europe
—our great risk, the treasure of our loneliness,

together and separate—coming at close of day
on walls the Cistercians
made an echo of the fog outside—dull, scouring whiteness . . .

Divorce was forgotten; passion
didn't exist. It was like wandering into
the dream before death, where everything is scoured

with a love like God's, because nothing one does any longer
affects it; the pain, now it's undemanding, radiant.
Writing poetry, one is free

—free for a moment—because one can hurl oneself
on that dream and still be alive.
(In that sense only, one writes instead of killing oneself.)

But, I say, *you can't live there. We move forward with*
whatever moves forward with us. If that goes dead,
moving forward with it, we go dead ourselves.

Then love becomes, incalculably, revenge . . .
But is that true? Is it reason enough? Our daughter
lives, this year, in books about the frontier,

Laura and Mary, blinding scarlet fever,
Indians appearing out of the flat horizon,
poison gas in the depths of the indispensable well . . .

You can see why: the danger simplifies.
Pa and Ma
won't look too long in each other's faces, calibrating

the terrible machinery; or into the neighbors' faces,
when they come by sled, perhaps once a winter,
and the Civil War ball gown is taken from its press.

Or were they wretched, and simply
afraid of the communal fear of using freedom?
Something is less simple than it ought to be . . .

Perhaps we both lacked courage,
preferring foregone disaster
to the terror of one single, limited thing.

Even—especially—in these last years
we'd rest on each other, sometimes,
when we suddenly came to peace from the long quarrels,

like swimmers
unable to move after hours in the dark lake;
or like *les Rois mages* of Autun, their crowns

so obviously too big for their one cape,
and the angel who wakes them with an almost shushing
gesture, as though true waking were still a sleep.

It seems so natural, now it will not happen
ever again. We leave it
as unbelieving

tourists leave a cathedral, half-relieved,
then sensing the heaviness isn't outside them but somehow
sinking endlessly through their veins . . .

There was a custom kept me
permanently too young, permanently old.
Life overarched and innocent—

how not feel losing it was half of death,
and the other half will never feel as
alien again?

Love and the Soul

Did you love her? I thought about her
continuously for a year. There were whole hours
there was nothing too thin about her look, her voice.

Did she love you? But it never counted against
any doubt or impulse of renunciation.

·

Only in the dark
could we listen clearly
to the voice that can say nothing but *I am good* . . .
I remembered Psyche, and how

I never wished to question
the god's masterful refusal to be known.
I had seen
too well, in their exact

afternoon light, the bright porticoes
which are the beloved, immaterialized;
and knew that, at midnight,
in the central chamber

what lifts the lamp, what tells her
anything she loves must be a monster
is not just "the human compulsion
to see, to know, the rejection

of whatever comfort derives from deception,"
but the soul's hatred and terror
of having all that depend
on the arbitrary contours of one flesh, one breath . . .

Another figure might be Stendhal's
of the branch
gathering crystals out of the cold water
at the bottom of a mine—

a girl drowned
in the shapeless, early depth within her man
the moment she takes on her specialness . . .
T. S. Eliot called requited love "the greater torment."

A man wanted to call the novel he never wrote that,
a man whose wife
kept dead mice and owls in the refrigerator,
to show just what they nourished each other by.

·

In what must be the misty, Northern
wandering of the story,
it is such small things—
a gold carding-comb, a gold thimble—

you are given with each failure,
each time you are told the place you want to go is
East of the Sun and West of the Moon . . .
But when the North Wind has spent itself and lies dying

having carried you to the castle
actually outside the universe,
it is these things that, given away,
let the soul enter; wake the beloved from false sleep . . .

Reading it out loud,
this morning of rejection,
I do not understand the story further.
I want it to be true;

not to have to believe
that what lights up the world from within is always the wrong thing;
that only struggle and limit
are the right.

Requited Love

1. Two People in Two Houses on a Hill

Il suo mister come mai, come mai fini?
Puccini, *La Rondine*

Two people in two houses on a hill,
the same record playing, think about a mystery.
The record asks how it will ever end.
They feel its end could go round the earth and the seas
and are puzzled it doesn't get them past the steps to
the bay window with its view, the untouched telephone . . .
The summer hangs fire. Those they live with enter the room,
and they have to know them, get this visibly
under something, back on a shelf. Then they think of driving,
the car going out of control at some numberless pylon,
not because they don't want life, and partly just for the smash of it,
but mostly the suspension, like the moment on *Folle amore*
when the notes should dip, but instead
the voice seems to fade, and another space enters the music,
as if their stasis meant another dimension floating
black hole or angelic transparence alongside
the unreal life. *Come mai, come mai fini?*

2. April and May

A space I leaned away into. A space with a name,
or at least an initial. (You made me destroy your letters.)
You flirted with everyone. But you and I felt
the same thing about each other, from the same instant.

We had small, silent agreements. Your place on my couch,
the garden end, near the white shades. That we always drank Scotch.
The "I miss you" on the phone—the most you would say—and answered,
when necessary, "likewise" or "me too."

I was never sure I loved your face. It was so unseizable,
the eyebrows not the same distance from the nose, in the photo,
brown eyes only bright at the rims. And then it was all of it
wholly home, like the flat friendly Southern voice.

A voice like clear alcohol: things came out thrilling,
with a silvery ring of unstated laughter,
though you never raised it. One outwaited its silences
without a clue, as one waited the blankness of your eyes.

                    •

Then there were things I will never write about.
I want them to be a part of life forever,
and like life—like our love—to vanish whole,
mouths stopped and stopped with the dust of incompletion.

Yet would spare the wheeze you gave, when I made you happy
in our balked embrace: half-torn from your lips, and yet deeply happy,
as if you belonged to the sky, and it had spoken
something of how it felt to light this particular

earth: the delta of freeways; hillside; dust . . .

And I grew a face I could love. The most paralyzed days
the tenderness of its eyes startled me, in the mirror
and my body moved easily in its small postures of grieving
through the distancing house. I felt this could none of it harm me.

But to whom could I give it? You would have said, to God,
whatever you meant by that—absolute, neutral love
for all that is incapable of consolation . . .
"Even if you lose me," you had said, "you'll have me."

But I needed to hear your voice. There was nothing I meant by God,
unless it was the questionless power that let
you empty my life—a space, yet arrived so completely
the moment we said I must give you up forever.

3. Wires at Inspiration Point

With less conscience, or more courage, would the earth
refuse them so, pushing them upward? High over Berkeley

she likes the metal giants striding the hills,
so delicate, yet strong; and when you stand beneath them

there's a kind of click, or blip, when a phone call passes . . .
—Are they telephone wires. he asks. I always thought they

carried the main power between towns.
—Oh, she says. But did you know

if there's a bird on the wire when you make a call, it isn't
electrocuted until someone answers.

•

—I had the fantasy you were inside me,
not just—you know—but all of you . . .

—The day I wanted you so much, I had the fantasy
I was you—my face your face, my hair your hair—

and all the while I went on desiring you. It's the same,
isn't it?

—Stop that. You're breaking the rules.

•

Coming back the same way, they both hear it, under the bird-jabber,
a short, keen rasp, like cicadas; and even cupping

his hand to his ear, he still thinks it comes from the grass . . .
But a quarter-mile on, when she says, *if the world ends*

we'll have had this, for people
like us, the end of the world is always near

the black wires fly straight above them
and he hears it this time: clearly, from the air.

4. Letter to Santa Fe

Staying over the three teaching days, to feel
our distance less: the aromatic dryness
when the heat recedes, the evening sprinklers going
on the desert-like, miniature-Midwestern lawns . . .
You like absences: will the high, wide air make you happy,
even after last week? Will N. be of help?
Will R. and E. take you to Bandelier,
where I climbed with my daughter to that smoke-hole, hardly
more than that, though a family lived or prayed there
(A. off somewhere, controlling her panic)—and felt the rock
stream back and back in itself, not knowing it meant how much in me
I didn't feel could come forward, not in this life.

About Cather: she has two themes, the empty land,
and love, always irregular, always balked.
Like a treble and bass line at the farthest distance
that can still be heard as dialogue. The emptiness
always opens; then some tiny space is reclaimed.
The doctor lights his quartz stove, to read and not go home.
A boy and girl trade toys on the planks of the general store.
(They will still be doing that on p. 250,
when her husband blasts them back to—emptiness.)

It's not fair to anyone, asking you to redeem
my steps there, two years back. It's too complex
why she was unhappy, and I was no help.
The red-earth dryness only told her how easily
one could die of thirst, that for me released an inner
fragrance in things. I think you and I could walk there,
our scrawny bodies somehow sure of carrying
enough in them to get us to the thin
stone lions almost shapeless with generations
of secret touching—overland pilgrims, by night.
And back? Or would we spoil it with our need

to be sure we had entered paradise? Too hard
to think of that now, or anything, when everything
seems to hinge on thought—
Love,

5. November and December

Last winter, before any of this started,
I used to think of you, waking up at three
and going to the bay window to console
yourself with its kingdom—three cities and the last ocean . . .
I thought if I were with you I could fathom
what made you unhappy, and feel what you felt, numbering
each light with its ring of pavement—beads of loneliness—
and you'd fall asleep, on the instant, on my breast.

If, at that hour, the phone rang once, then stopped,
I'd lie awake after, certain
you'd let yourself just dial, somehow knowing . . .

•

This fall, you want to watch me asleep;
it seems, you say, so unlike me. You are disappointed;
sleep eludes me by your side, the way our X-ray
speech escapes from normal conversation,
leaving us still
half-strangers when we talk of the day, the bread.

And your body, that's somehow held
such freedom for me, such rest—
isn't its childlike spareness
a strange blue jewel, closing on itself
in your quick, shallow sleep?

And then the night, with its violent, disembodying voices . . .

After the disco closes,
the black man's voice, searching the street's thinness
like the ring of a fallen trashcan lid: *You've got*

to choose between us . . .
And the voice that finally answers him, so quiet
sexless and far away—
a casual passerby? The hour I doze
it's your voice, shouting back at an accuser.

If my love is not full love,
what use to me are the stars, those helpless fountains?
Even as a child
I was afraid of the thought of them, like a clockhand, angling
all night past the black roofs . . .

I've wanted the moments
to stitch us together, in blood and nearness,
till I hardly knew your name—in a pause like sleep,
where our gradualness could at last be told from failure . . .

And in the morning, when the machine of me gives up trying
and looks out, your eyes, that seem to hold the weariness
for both of us
are open, watching: "You were possuming."

6. The Puccini Record Again, after a Year

In the life even now unbreakable, under glass,

we three sit and hear the bad soprano
falter through the *O to me descended
down from the throne of most high*

paradise—a wave in the sky, twice climbing
its fourths and sevenths, twice falling too low, then circling
back to the unresolving not-quite-center . . .

It's sung to her child, before going
behind the screen; but including
how love and Fate descended

in the same unsearchable, centerless wave . . .
You had trouble getting used to it, how the smallest
things were sung, not spoken; you still the outsider—scattered

imbalances of an opera evening with
a couple, new friends . . . (Your coughdrops. The plastic
champagne glass whose bottom somehow unscrewed and spilled.)

Two months later the violet in your eyes' dull brown
gathered for me; and what in another person
would have been a clear look, shook there

violently for the almostness. And for a year—
a wave in the sky—the past that did not happen
was allowed to happen: the high school breathlessness;

the *I can't imagine we have different thoughts;* your standing
outside my house at night, not caring about past or future,
hardly wanting to come closer than the wind . . .

How, from that, to "this sense of failing you
every minute I'm with you . . ."
Music, we know, is always bigger

than a person. That's why there are those Cupids
on proscenium arches, reclining
in a space no foot could climb to, and no hand

touch, across air . . . Could you have flung yourself
like a long high C, and not had some lack of gravity
that would suddenly turn away, find it not worth trying,

and writing, in your classroom cursive, "miss
the good times," for fear of giving anything
legibly cancel the "miss," and put "remember."

A note too high was struck, and a house vanished;
a note too high was struck, and a life vanished,
even to the white cloth shades

I liked to place you under, the mild
clear nights of that paralyzed winter, so your hair
would play on the luxury of their odd brocade.

In our last weeks together, I actually wished for
the next life you believed in,
where I saw your eyes were clear, and able to hold . . .

There's no good reason, no
resolution. Close-ups of singers
are always disturbing: the whole face

skewed by the exaggerating, naked pleasure
of the enormous mouth—
unlike actors, who can present

the desirable, because they always watch who's watching back . . .
—Safe in our house that night, after you drove home,
she said, *You always know*

someone will die bloodily, that's what
gives it its keenness. And though I might have said, no,
it's the unspeakable value, the icon of love,

that makes her death
itself the tragedy—nothing more said or sung—
it's sheer luck no one died from all of this.

No one took from it more
than one carries through death: although
I seem to have been given, permanently, the tears

that surprised me so
when I came back to you, out of doubt and distance;
that moved you so much

you leaned down and licked one off my face.

Fragments: Traveling in Marriage

1. The Etruscan Couple in the Villa Giulia

They have not shown themselves as lovers; neither
as dark-winged Fates to each other.

That's how the young couple knew they were theirs, the moment
they approached them, down separate, angling corridors:
turned a little aside from each other, the man too thin
for his great height, and a faint irony curling
his lip forever; the woman ample, settled
in the glow of baked earth, in the four talkative braids.

They have not died from knowing each other; they show it
by lifting the cup encouragingly
to the invisible friends who never leave them,
whom they've persuaded
to stay so late, that even these two have slipped
out of the glass and taxicabs of Rome
to hear their last story, and catch the fine
familiar reflex with which
she takes the last sentence from his lips, to end it—

who perhaps, in the dark to come, will love each other
at last wholly, forgiving: a red-earth glow.

2. Landfall

Peace of weary-edged tenderness. They choose a house.
How hard for each of them to live. Respect goes on forever.
The inset benches, the brick patio, the strange stalks
brown-bare, then all white flowers, then bare again. Like England
or old age, so carefully made. You couldn't leave it
if you wanted to, because you couldn't finish counting
what there is to leave: snowdrops suddenly
outside the January study window, gnats climbing their narrow
invisible ladder, when there's enough dusk in the air . . .
And so they do what they can: argue the pictures
to the almost right place on the wall, and scrape the moss
from the brick's almost facial weathering, so the deck chairs
can go out on it, so that one day a quiet-mannered
visitor will come and her child spill her odd, unflowery
perfume playing with her purse in the Craft-style bathroom.

II

Deb's Dream about Pavese

I.

He had a long red scarf shielding his throat
(looking the way he does in the last photo)
and it scared you, because it was fire-colored, and like a snake.
But he said (in Italian, but you understood),
Take it, it will take the fever away;
so you gathered as he unwound, and woke up better.

To me he says, *One nail drives out another*
but four nails make a cross.
I will be a diabolical friend to her.
We are given only what we ask for with indifference.
The thing most feared in secret always happens.

He says in the wastefulness
of going from person to person, the feelings
never in balance, the universe
slides off toward extinction—a man
no more than the rumpled smells of his
unacceptableness. Only a fool
clings then to the look he had to
misinterpret. And the woman
is as helpless as the man. (His anger is that
of total Need. Does he know
if it were less absolute, his prick would stand?)

I cannot refute him. But something healed you.

2.

If it were that old story
of searching for the other half of you through the world,
the odds wouldn't be good, but there'd be a logic—
but it's more like
the body of Osiris, one right thing glimmering
in each person, as if swallowed by mice or fish . . .

—It could go another way. To bed too quickly,
with lots of giggling. Later she's sensible, "slow," her coolness
hurts him; or she's sure
he'd be bored in the end. And still, it's a little marriage,
describing the moonlight, waking up early to wind,
coming home at night to camomile tea.

—*In New York now a lot of people are almost
asexual. Disease and, I don't know, the meeting people . . .*

Because all loves are not the one love they are meaningless.
Because all loves are the one love they are real.

I see the scarf, where it curves through all of them,
like DNA, like Isis finding
here the clear look, there the touch that grazes
and gives your skin back its childhood softness, though it goes—
the story longer told to each new person, but each time
told by someone different, each
time a window . . . (*But when
does one get to what one holds to, what one doesn't lose?*)
I must pick it up, where he threw it in the dirt,
the pointless cellular chain.

The Minoan Distance

Say you could have come there from Athens, when its empire
started to fade, fleeing the guilts of that, the shortages,
or other things—a wife, the poets
suffering the exactions of their choliambi—
and found it unchanged (unlikelier things have happened,
a palace torched by volcanoes beyond the sea) . . .
—found the wild-beast colors in the porticoes,
and the conversations you imagined, airier, less tightened
on taxes and the weather, less convinced
that fate must bind in tighter with every year . . .
Would it have consoled you?—the constant brightness woven
into everything, the brighter, earlier gods . . .
The children take such an early part in the Mysteries,
and the grown-ups watch them, as if they were the Mystery.
No one despises the rich, or their own greed
for money; no one despises laborers, either.
(There was a painter who stopped for five years and learned the bull-leaping.
When he came back, his colors were somehow bloodier,
as though done from beneath the skin.) The hardest thing
to get used to is the women: how they walk
the streets with their breasts bare, under-cinched with gold;
how even the shrewdest believe the fortune-tellers,
the masseuse who describes the colored auras rising
from each organ as her fingers approach it, drawing the star-map
of their most cosmic fate.

And if the middle-aged ones
get still more beautiful, leathery, wise as cats,
explaining you to yourself like the sun
turning on some pretty thing of angled crystal . . .
—You cannot explain to them
that leaving her in Athens, one with its quarrels,
was not a "process," that smiling roller-coaster leaving you
predeterminedly clean at the end, but the slow undying
attrition of an affection that is no longer useful,
but not less real.
In the books they read all day, about how to live,
the greatest sin is depending on, doing too much for, others.
(It is all right to depend entirely on the gods.)
When you're with them, it's the transparent
universe; when it's over,
they'd show their new friend at a party at your mother's,
and think they loved you while they were doing it; and apologize
in a hurt voice, like a caught child, your perspective
too big or small to fit themselves inside it—
not their "needs"; not the great sky where all are shadows . . .
In the end, they prefer their own, who understand this.

Domestic Architecture

There is no reason to be unhappy. Purplish flowers
star the twigs out your window; it has a stately frame,
eight small panes in procession above the great one,
brown mullions like musical bars. And if the neighborhood's
not what you asked for, still . . . Such things have woken you
at almost every age; what is there more?
But your life was unarraigned then, protected by others,
and the day moved inside that, in its small panes.
And if what protected also imprisoned, made a sameness?
Now the first hope is gone, you'd say you did it
for honesty: to say what you meant about longing,
not half-adapt to one you were still half-failing,
and so be taller; so, perhaps, break open
what was knotted inside . . . Now, your lover brings strangeness
like many jewels on the dressertop overnight.
You are trying to build each other a shelter in the larger
spaces of your hearts. You don't feel safe for an hour.
There are so many gaps that can open. When she sees
the cracks in the ceiling and not the stately window;
when you see the ranch-house blankness and not the elm
she turns to, waking, the wind has a chance to start blowing
that says birth to death is a single plain; there was never
a house on it, not a tree, not a pluckable purple flower.

Wide-Angle Shot:
Return to Snowy River

When she leaves her father for him, the landscape changes—
the incredible drop-offs at their feet, the pointed
after pointed ranges, near-bald with stones—

aren't just a way of not showing sex, its monumental
suspensions the body sometimes expresses, sometimes not,
oddly aslant the heart;

but pure portrait of contact, pure portrait of danger,
and the old claim, that all of life is in that,
the infinite stopped at its feet . . .

It's clearly all we have yet: contact, risk;
though love, as always, finds odd nails to hang
itself on—yogurt for breakfast, the ironing board . . .

Little stammerer, your monumental
silences before the downdraft of these things,
and what boils up from them always, the unlovely

intractable *I*—cliffside
paths I wander with you as if they were the years
from your age to mine, loving what endangers me . . .

Then your words hooked, torn—lone eagles—over depth—

The Ambivalent Man

He works so hard to make each moment perfect,
but underneath there's always

a kind of negative forming, to be developed
in the salt of his solitude; an accuser saying

everything she said was boring or mean-spirited,
he was never comfortable with her for an instant.

Of course, she may simply be the wrong person.
There are always reasons
anyone he would choose is the wrong person.

·

Was that why—their first walk
out on the pier, the day choppy, facing the ocean—

she spoke of the courage
of those who once set out on it, in their creaking boats?

·

When all he can want to say is *stop it stop it,*

he thinks of what he would like
to be happening instead,

and sees himself lay his head
on her bare shoulder,
and have her understand something
from so far back, he can only catch the blue
edging toward lavender—
and not words, just a series of enlarging silences . . .

And then he thinks perhaps this *was* the memory:
the eye-path crossed and went elsewhere, the receiving face
could no longer be known, or loved.

.

But what, when the nerves, that make the words misfire
between them
are the very thing that, watching her cross a room—

that tissue of hesitations, flinch at being visible,
plus a certain doggedness, as if
her face were having to push a heavy boulder—
he sees with his whole body, he's way inside
like being inside a tree.

.

She says, *the anglerfish,*
because the male not only spawns but lives
inside the great, glistening, open globe
of the female's vagina . . .

When he feels right about her,
people mountains trees
all slip back into their right, beautiful place.

•

He thinks if he could make her a gift
even of the pain she is in him. That's why he chooses

the statue of the convulsed man, half-emerging
from the body of a frog; that's

why he leaves
the copy of Kafka face down on the table.

•

She has learned not to trust the tears
that well in his eyes, as if
seeing had become a warmer, closer thing . . .

They say he is too happy to have persuaded himself;
they say he will say anything
just to go on being there, in the moment, one.

•

She will tire of it, in the end.
That way, he will still be the victim.
He will never be the one who has rejected someone.

•

She will go by his apartment to pick up something.
He is playing Madame Butterfly; it sounds as if
it has been playing for days.
But what he says is, I do better alone.

•

And what if the negative tells the truth?
—Tells him he's come to something
known long ago, meager
and dark to itself beneath the
apparent sweetness?
What if his kindness was only
an old complicity
with his own undoing,
his estrangement the saving lamp?

•

Or, he steps out onto it.
That metaphor. Bridges. Ships.
The ground giving one way or another
at every move.
The constant ringing—does everyone hear it,
making things strange as a dream?
He doesn't know if he's bored. He is very scared.
He takes another step.

Forest Street

So what if, days after, he couldn't look into faces,
and the morning light was itself a face, an eyelike moistness
beading, if it came early, the knobs of his poor chairs,
driving him back into dark, his sheets like downward wings . . .

And if someone told him C. S. Lewis's heaven
was like that, *so sharply real*
it would hurt the feet of the damned,
he would know he could marry, needing that balance,
that insistence on reality, so his body
could stand with another body, in the light.

For what else was there?—the bars' delusion,
all eyes and no eyes, the slipping-space between creatures,
the night-cool breathing
its waver into the air, at ten in the morning . . .

But there was something else: a cry, true distance?

It's not that the loneliness was part of it—
the almost accidental girl, the round
red rug of the summer rental—
still there, I walked past it this year, in the stick-storm of Cambridge Victorian—

but without the loneliness he wouldn't have felt it,
not, at any rate, at that age—

in her slipperiness the endless interval,
the *tender indifference,* as if a traveler
should pass, once only,
through a street all shined gray stone in the early morning . . .

And when it's all gone, every face disassembled
from these addresses, what's there might be what he felt
after, in the real street, passing the islanded streetlamps—
under light bright as paint, translucent pulp of leaves;
under the real paint of the garages, wood
and the watery flicker of rot, wood that would again be earth—
something his body discovered
it was part of, something that went down
within itself forever
and vanished there.

Rilke's Argument with Don Giovanni

I never thought
I'd be anything like you . . .
I was drawn up, as in a whirlwind, by their gaze
and wished to live there forever—a soul around my soul—
astonished, perhaps, to be wanted there at all—

who was Mitzi in the army; the boy fainting by the wall at school.

But then, when the wincing *not right*
began in my head; when I wanted
so much to be loved in the moment I found my separateness
still there, still real—I needed
the one who could be told anything, even the thing
that drove her away.

People will say I disliked the body; it's the easiest
explanation, for someone who talked with angels.
But my dear ones will know something different,
how astonished and careful
I could be, like a boy
given something unbelievable,
the pale gold flare at the bottom of the stream.

The men of our time burst into them
like the brusk hussar
at the dressing-room door in Strauss's *Ariadne.*

I loved their talents
as if they were my own talent,
a surer hand to reach the brush, the page—
transfixed with knowing
how a child shapes itself, will-less, in the dark.

And they must have felt something heavy in me, too rich,
too complete in itself. They dreamed
stronger dreams in my presence.
But the weight was what sank, what even I couldn't hold.

I always hoped the right one
would arrive like wind,
that freshly, instantly touching everywhere.
I never remembered
the nature of wind is to pass by.

I'm glad to think of their oval portraits in my biography,
soul on soul on soul,
clouds and clouds of them, lace and hairpins—
and I whose soul could vanish
at a spastic's tic on a curb's edge in Paris.

I pray they weren't what yours were—
things
flung in the face of the echoing man of stone.

The Moments

If I were like the people
whose moments of pure love are strong enough
for the places designed to receive them:
the seaside hotel room, arranged with fruit and flowers . . .
Mine wouldn't have the courage—
mine would be the accidental things, the first conversations,
giddy, and *spared,* with not having needed to happen.
Mine would be the loft bedroom
where I shouldn't have been at all, and you wouldn't be, for long,
looking down—*so far down*—at the embers of our fire;
then the long cold stairway down to the shower in the morning.
Naked, out of bed, it was clear you were slightly taller,
and some protective impulse,
for all your skittishness,
made you push me into the center of the warm water.
Later I got out
and sang softly to myself while you turned it to cold.
Then we snuck in separately to breakfast with the others.

Your Forest-Moonlight Picture

Unbroken sea surface, swelling and changing,
as if a small plane were scanning it—breathing mists,
breathing pure paint, slash and shimmer, and no horizon;
or star-material, roiling, metal, gray . . .
Then the mute funny thing you'd drift above it,
ball-bearings, rope, a bicycle, an O—
never explaining, nothing linking down.
For a few days it was our forest, the sea was moonlight—
hunter's moon—before as well as behind it,
and real black branches you could be lost or found in . . .
Then I was gone; the surface was repainted
hard sea, the branch, like Dante's, grew small thorns . . .
You watched me all the way down the road from your door,
as if I couldn't help getting smaller and smaller.

Toward the New Year

(Lower Manhattan)

1.

The sharper numbers slipping upward. Rains
leach a whole past of snow
from the black streets. Weightless acceptance,
though the bridges still tear the long perspectives upward
like iron muzzles, of some afterworld . . .
—How could a whole city be washed of such
love, of such terror?
(And the man in the subway, flattering, peddling his roses—
but no one has said *your wife*
of any of the others . . .)

2.

But they won't stop rising . . . Lying down at last, between
"necessary" and "not permanent"—and how much farther
the night might drift us, even when exhaustion
shelved us like twin rock strata underground . . .
Was it the way the sirens sifted upward
(the firehouse roofs below), floors, rungs past our high bed,
made me see them as rising through, above us—
numbers like dawn birds, more and more, till they stop, taller,
whiter than cities, with our separate names.

Unanticipated Mirrors

(In Memory of Alfred Satterthwaite)

1.

Leave the doors open, the poet says, *the whole house*
open all night, so we may die
a little here, in us, and there in him
we live a little. Before anyone died here
this house stood open. I could see from the darkness
Isabel and her sister shelling peas
at either end of the long walnut table.
She told me I should work for a newspaper that summer,
how she'd loved that—the glimpses into other lives . . .
The weak light hung cloudy, pregnant, in the dark wood,
as if a house could be the summer night
brought indoors, flickerings, blowings-back of white
curtains, unanticipated mirrors.
Then Alfred came downstairs, and brought my story.

2.

Why wasn't I angry? He said just what my father
might have said: you couldn't tell, I might fail as a writer,
I'd still make a good scholar . . . Out of the depth of leafage
an explanation presses, a signature like the wound
in the horse-chestnut flower. I was living that sense

that even—especially—unhappy love gives
of seeing things twice; seeing for the absent other.
And in that double sight, I saw the failure
was his, and was not evil; ploughed back under
into—what?—as the night-smell takes back everything—
the open doors, the glass in his hand, the eyebrows'
Mephistophelean dance over the eyes' pure, black
astonishment at life . . . And saw, too, that my seeing
might be plowed under; or, in me, live and grow.

3.

To pass into a house, as into a mirror;
to see what the grown-ups wouldn't show us, the wrestling
with their own pasts, with each other, the dignity down—
fighting us too, often enough, fleeing the ghosts
of unwritten books . . . but accepting our chaos too, our failure.
So it's always a little the house in detective stories,
in the candlelight after the great crime, when faces—
even one's own, especially the beloved's—
yaw and flicker into unsearchableness.
And it has its real ghost, a young one, I've feared and hoped
to meet again, these open-windowed nights; who lived here
when he failed his Comps and his father threw him out,
two years before he fell/jumped? under the train,
So *Grave. Wilderness.* (More poets.) But also *Paradise.*

4.

In the detective stories, too, we turn
to some opposite of the Father—
some cocaine mainliner, some grim divorcé
or fat man (even too-perfect Lord Peter

has his shellshock; the story requires an almost
unmanning)—to show, by the light of his funny pain,
where evil is: not where the Fathers said, in the moment
we forgot their existence, suddenly only ourselves;
but the slower loneliness when that isn't somehow
caught back, accepted, until one chilled heart
thinking it only calculates, revenges . . .
I felt my life balance among other lives—
the shape of an adulthood we could enter
without maiming ourselves.

5.

Dick's been cleaning this house for weeks—the fireplace ashes
you just threw, these last years, at the foot of the cellar stairs,
you'd given up so . . . and the suicide letter
in case Isabel died first—but addressed *to* Isabel . . .
And *So what,* at the last, we sit here saying.
You gave us, I said when you died, chaos and warmth,
the mystery of their balance. When Joel's father
tracked him here at last—I can hear it in your mouth—
"He was standing in the front doorway, and he said,
'I should have beaten him more, when he was a child'—
and he could have had me to court then, easily—
I said, 'Dr. ——, you are a son of a bitch.'"
And so released us; for the young always know they're
murderers, if only of their pasts.

6.

And if we too served your needs—wounded relivings
of youth, escape from work, from the loving war with each other—
So what, we say again. *The house must be left open,*

the poets have said it, *the tower built without stones.*
The thin walls of this house are old. A farmer set these
orchard trees out in the huge planetree dark
that makes the nights so endless. I like to think
his stern God lost himself and then came back
in this quicksilver loosing of the boundaries—
the young not young, the old not old, but life
flaring in its quick resin on itself,
one clear thing like the round-filled glass of sherry,
chaos that keeps the circle unconfining—
the smoke-breath lasting, hosts and guests asleep.

Enthusiasm

Someone said, *your poems lack enthusiasm,*
and was afraid half the story
would die of that. So I went back
to Charlottesville, five paces north from the fireplace,
faint-fragrant in the hot weather, then west into
the cramped dining-room, as if that would bring me to us
practicing the modes of caring
our hands still knew as one, in spite of our minds—
in from bedding out marigolds in the clingy clay,
or sitting together, the long afternoon,
rounding and rounding the small, egg-shaped pieces,
orange carrot, pale turnip, for *navarin printanier.*
There would be white straight rain and sudden thunder,
it being Virginia, it being summer,
so that later, in the cool, the dining-room table transported,
largesse of candles and friends on the screen porch, into the dark . . .
And next day come so soon, *day falling through day through the screen door* . . .
And so autumn: the heavy pear orchard of the stars;
the birdseed bright as salt on the rare ice,
and seven purple finches; the robin on the first of March;
the ashtree that was our guardian and the moonlight
you wanted to stay out in, for your poem
where it walked through the houses and left them all one house,
transparent, unthreatened; and I, too often, nervous
of trying to hold the moment, dragged you in.

Fire and Flood

(Charlottesville)

You wake to thunder, before you can name it, happy:
that falling in air, like a musical note breaking crystal;
horizons pacing, mountains learning to fly.
You say to yourself, this could kill people, burn down houses,

but the happiness grows . . . Then the rain sets down,
the endless whisper absorbs the creaking of floors
until nothing is strange anymore—like a new
kind of daylight, that's cobwebby, and passes through things.

And if you read next day of tornadoes, and thirty dead
three states to the West—undeniably the night
will freshen still more . . . Is it love of
destruction then, with the old *The Lord has spared me?*

Or breaking rules, like sticking your hand in the fire?
Or a world unmade, gone fluid? When nothing
holds its place, everything blossoms: no one more welcome
than the unexpected guests in the flood year . . .

No one is more at peace than a small boy after a fire,
coming home in the dark, to the improvised meal out of cans;
or after an earthquake—out West—seeing the old kerosene
lantern brought out, like a little hunched god on the table.

Highway Restaurant

We all have places we step out of time and are perfectly happy.
This is one of mine. Perhaps because it's a place
where I can be grown-up yet have my childhood,
or because it took me so long to feel good in public alone,
without self-consciousness, chattering in my head,
that even looking at the bad mural with the mileages
to the cities, even lifting my water glass, is fun.
We all choose people in such places, though we feel we like everyone;
I choose the young waitress
who thinks her nerves are part of the other life, and invisible,
and doesn't see what spare beauty they give each moment, here;
and the man—they're about thirty—so obviously pleased to be with the woman,
though she's fleshy and somehow sick—anyway, takes pills before dinner.
And I think I know, apart from whoever *I'm* missing,
why I choose them. They're riding rip-currents of the present;
they say we're in our flesh, our nerves, as in a river,
and it may take years to master—or it may drown us tomorrow.
And I've heard today that a man I've respected, but never known well,
has a form of cancer with 20 percent chance of survival.
And though it would be very foolish, defensive, and tempting fate
to say I don't care how many more years I live,
that's like what I feel. The highway is a river,
exhaustion in it is beautiful, and our gathering here—
so much larger somehow, almost family—
has something of a fast-forward of all the gathering
and losing in our lives.

You can't quite say it: the joy comes from somewhere,
and while that doesn't prove we'll ever
wake up in a different river, in the sky,
it just might prove there's an object equal to joy,
and if we don't hold it any one place, it's only because it needs
so much to be everywhere . . .
Like the waitress. How I'm too shy to say more to her
("More coffee?" "Please." A good sunset's over,
the long, flimsy curtains drawn . . .)
but when I go up with the check the girl at the cash register
sees her scrawl on the back and says, "Lisa Ann. She's *fun!*"

For My Daughter, Leaving

Dearest, I would not want you to forget
this place, though it was never home to me
till too much drama made that not the question . . .
Palms and winter camellias; the seasonlessness gathering
to the ocean-light focus of the winter solstice;
the Craft tiles with florets and knights in armor;
or even the street where I moved, its flat-glare bungalows . . .
The schools where you learned so much about Native Americans,
so little after 1790; the summer trips north with Grandma
to the long white twilights, the brother-killer-whale,
the ratty spruce drooping and stretching, the whole coast curving
round, like its own looped makings, to Japan.
To tragedy, serenity. Balance unlike our world,
its *happiness,* its *failure.* Which were we?
Puzzles gathered dust on the hall table. Before
we had a vacuum cleaner, before the crumbling
undercarpet was up from the one room I lived in,
we had fish. They swam so far beneath us—
your stoic face; my distracted anguish about women—
we could hardly guess their ills. Then one had dropsy,
its intestines came out through its anus and wouldn't go back.
I learned, that day, how you put down a fish.
You stun it in cold water, then wrap it up
in wet kleenex, so it won't suffocate,
then put it in the freezer.
That way it just dozes off, the pet stores say.

When you found out what I'd done, we had to rewrap him
in a Christmas cookie tin, with herbs and ribbons.
That was the beginning of the Goldfish Graveyard.
Even daubed on with white house-paint—"Princess
a special fish," "Silverstreak," "Little Arrow,"
"Good Fish"—this one a mass grave, short-lived prizes
from a school fair—their names didn't last the rainy season.
But a garden of worn bricks sprang up amid the thyme
and free-landing poppies; mint; ineradicable blackberry;
the tramped-down paths making a tiny center.
You could never quite tell how people would respond.
Most girlfriends liked it, but one of the kindest
called it Auschwitz for fish. You could see her point—
a culture, like so much in culture, built on
the premise of small things neglected till they died.
But she was the one who gave us Lumpy,
the only fish who rises to his name.
She hadn't fed him much, so he just kept growing
until someone else told me about a goldfish
that ended up a foot long, and I got careful.
(She hadn't named him, either. His twin, Bumpy, died.)
I pray he will never lie here, his tail will bend,
too big for the cramped corners, but a sign of
something—a flowing, a freedom—when I
have moved him to newer, airier rooms; when you
come back from the sharp autumns of your new city.

Tidepools

How near the shore the blue
gathers again in the water after breaking,
cobalt and electricity in the clearness . . .

But withheld now, upending these
little homes, little bits of the inner salt of daylight,
separate a few hours so we can see

that first idea of flesh, the sponge's
live carpet on the inner face of rock,
touch and play-flinch from the devouring flowers . . .

How grave and attuned your small face gets,
so I also see, without blame or forgiveness,
what it was not in my clouded look to mend.

Yet you seem to like me best here, crossing
the high-tide island, its wave of uninhabited grasses,
saying, *Daddies are good at outdoor things.*

And we hold the names together, *chiton, nudibranch,*
as they rose, once, from the page
in the aromatic shore house, in the desklamp's pincer,

Blake's icicle of Creation, passionless
as the light is, also, for the man returning
from all the journeys; from the journey of knowing fate.

2.

When the second life came from within my body,
at fourteen, fifteen—how I hated this; how I wanted
the Midwest opening

its joyful elm towns
to our returning journey,
like crossed swords above the joyful bride and groom;

its humid light in which things grew so densely
it seemed space could curl inside itself forever
and a birdcall still shoot through, unimpeded—

like a life filled with friends and saying more
unguardedly right than you thought the day had room for,
and more always to step out of the stillness;

and as the small creatures know they move more safely
for the infoldings,
so at night the dancers, unimpeded,

hardly feeling the need to touch each other . . .
It seemed then one could be mixed with something unknown
but unbetrayable.

It seemed there was an act that was a preparing for death,
and the crickets knew it, with their intermitted
falterless ratchet, down by the grass-stems, near autumn . . .

The moment would come, after years, when they would catch me—
brimming, then stopping; without
measure, without doubt—and the explanation of the world

couldn't hold me more.
They seemed to say, *you have not done your preparing;*
but it is only one action, so there is always time.

3.

Suzuki Roshi
says if you could think with a frog's mind,
through and through,

you would be Buddha.
But what unremitting steadiness
of wind the cormorants know themselves by, plunging

to their guano island . . .
Do seals feel warm or cold?
And Steinbeck's "tidepool Johnnie,

growing weak and perhaps
sleepy as the searing digestive acids
melt him down . . ."

—A friend perhaps dying. Transparency
through which childhood
shows more, its sadness

never wholly readable . . .
(Was it because it was lonely,
or you knew, even then, it would end?)

And the midwinter light
that beats up so low, but sharp, off the ocean's mirror,
the headlands velvety,

translucent with new green: as if that light
took them up with both hands
to give back to the sun.

4.

I haven't mentioned my father's grave,
a few sand dunes away, where every second
or third visit you, who never knew him,

like to place the smoky-purple flowers . . .
If *a child's life*
is punishment for the father's—the slow turning

outward of the wounds that he kept hidden,
but more grotesque now, so that reason cannot help one
live around them, not

live them through; and not through healing when we die . . .
What will hold then (not, surely, the comforting
map of the years, the "successes")

against the glare
pouring in from farther than we can imagine,
salt plants enduring it, killdeer alighting?

But the vastness is in us, too, the rising and falling.
When I have managed to forget
everything but my breath, the story has touched me

at all points at once, its clangors
and bright screens.
                              I used to envy the dead
in urban graveyards, in summer,

for how much life swam back
in on their dark: a car horn
in the street, the shiny fence-hafts, the humid elms . . .

If I love someone enough
I might end there, or anywhere, losing my self
in a place that is *ours,* an endlessly inland.

If not, I am willing to be salt and sand.

Notes

"Love and the Soul." The lines in quotation marks are taken, with permission, from Louise Gluck's wonderful essay, "The Dreamer and the Watcher." The "man whose wife/kept dead mice and owls in the refrigerator" was the critic R. P. Blackmur.

"Deb's Dream About Pavese." The italicized lines in the second stanza are taken, somewhat randomly, from Pavese's diaries (*This Business of Living*, Quartet Books, 1980).

"Unanticipated Mirrors." The "poet" is Juan Ramón Jiménez, "Dejad las puertas abiertas" (*The Penguin Book of Spanish Verse*, p. 425). The "more poets," roughly paraphrased, are Shelley ("Adonais") and Hart Crane ("The Broken Tower").

"Tidepools." "Steinbeck's 'tidepool Johnnie'" is from *Cannery Row*, Chapter VI.

DATE DUE

SEP 03 2008			